# Dance into an Inner Light
## Journeys into your Inner Sources of Power

Birgit Baader

translated from the original German
by Charlotte C. Milstein

**TONECOLORSPACE**

For Julie and Noa

# Contents

# Welcome!

<table>
<tr><td>E tu kahikatea</td><td>upright as the kahikatea tree</td></tr>
<tr><td>Hei whakapai uru roa</td><td>we stand and grow together</td></tr>
<tr><td>Awhi mai awhi atu</td><td>care for me, care for you</td></tr>
<tr><td>Tatau tatau e.</td><td>together we ARE.</td></tr>
</table>

This *waiata,* a prayer sung by the Maori, shows us how closely tied we are to nature – it paints a picture of the unity from which our life force and joie de vivre originate.

The meditations in this book are inspired by the primal energies found in nature. The animal and plant kingdoms, the birds and the sea dwellers, the ancient ferns and many other tree friends; but also the children of fire, water, and wind, the minerals and many others gave them their *mauri* (life force) and their *wairua* (spiritual energy).

*Everything that lives can tell us something about itself in its own language.*
*You just have to know how to listen and to understand.*

Our strength lies in our connection with the essence of all things; the light of life. The meditation exercises in this book create a place in which we can connect to this light and find new strength, concentration and balance.

The illustrations help with visual immersion. The soft, round forms and colors have their own effect and radiate a powerful tranquility.

In Maori *Turuki whakataha* means, "Set all things aside that disturb your peace." This is what we wish to achieve with this book and the book and the corresponding audio CDs (see Appendix).

*Welcome to an exciting journey*
*into your inner worlds!*

**Motueka, Aotearoa/New Zealand**

# Active Meditations

The following meditations are good for when you are restless or don't feel like sitting still or lying down. You can also use them as an introduction for one of the fantasy journeys in the following chapters. They are fun and connect you with your inner source of power from which you can draw courage, new ideas, calmness, and trust. They help you with decisions, when you don't know what you should do, when you are sad, feeling alone or misunderstood. They help you "flow" and let the energy flow freely throughout your body. Other than the walking meditation, you can do all of the meditations lying down, for instance when you are sick and have to stay in bed. However, I recommend that if it's possible, you go to one of your favorite spots outside in nature. The energy outside in the fresh air helps you to come into contact with your inner sources of strength and power.

You can close your eyes or leave them open, whichever you prefer. Do the meditations for as long as they help you. In the beginning, this may only be a few minutes. When you have had more practice, you may decide to dance in the light longer.

# Rhythm Meditation

For this meditation, you need a drum or another rhythm instrument; preferably one that resonates nicely and creates a deep sound.

Get comfortable, if possible with your back straight so that the energy can flow freely through you. When you are ready, start softly playing a rhythm. Let yourself go; the rhythm will come on its own.

If you are going on the journey with several people, it may take a while before you all play together in harmony.

Take your time. Just observe how the sounds differ from each other. Some may be loud and dominant, others softer and tentative, some strong and rhythmical, others uneven and wavering. Let your hands and your body find your own rhythm; one which flows easily and with which you feel comfortable and familiar.

If you have been on this drumming journey more often and you know your own rhythm, you can start experimenting with different rhythms and volumes. Let yourself go; try it louder, softer, weaker, stronger, faster, slower… Perhaps you can feel your heartbeat and drum along to it for a while. Or feel the heartbeat of Mother Earth – slow, full of peace and strength… You can feel it best if you sit or lie directly on the ground in a meadow or the woods.

If you are outside, you will, in time, feel many different rhythms and play in unison with them. Air, water, fire, earth – they all have their own rhythms and it is fun to play together with them, to get to know other rhythms and learn to play them, and then practice your own rhythm together with the others. Before you play with others, however, whether with other people or other creatures or elements, it is important that you have found your own rhythm and know how it feels so that you do not lose yourself in their rhythms and so that you can always draw from yourself and your own strength!

Your rhythm may also change over time. You can always recognize it because it seems to flow "all by itself" from your hands, and you feel good, strong and light while playing it.

# Toning

Get comfortable and sit or lie so that your whole body, especially your stomach, is free and relaxed. Personally, I am best able to do this meditation outside in nature: on the beach or in the forest under the trees, sitting cross-legged or in the lotus position. In the beginning, it might help if you find a place where you can be completely alone and no one can hear you so that you can stay entirely within yourself and let your sounds flow freely from you.

When you are ready, breathe in deeply and consciously and while breathing out, let tones flow out of you with your mouth slightly open.

Be aware of where the tones come from. Are they coming from deep within your stomach? Or from your throat? Or from your head? Are they deep? Or high?

After a while, when you are completely relaxed and loosened up, you may feel your entire stomach area vibrate and resonate as the sounds rise from deep within. Your entire body resonates like the body of a guitar. Allow yourself to be one with the sounds and play with them.

The sounds can connect you with your inner "gut feeling." This deep inner source of power goes far beyond your knowledge and the information in your mind and your memories. Within this center, you will find many valuable answers and information about yourself, your path and others.

Perhaps you will discover that the sounds are coming from your head or your throat if you are tense, stressed or annoyed. The deeper from within you they come, the closer you are to your center, your inner source of power.

Play with your sounds whenever you are nervous, indecisive, upset, or "in a bad mood" – or simply to learn a bit more about yourself and have fun.

# Singing Bowl Meditation

Get comfortable. Lay the singing bowl on your open palm, on a firm pillow or on your stomach (if you are lying on your back). Use the mallet to get the bowl singing and listen to the sound.

Do you feel the light shiver of the sound on your hand or body?

How does the sound change?

How many breaths does the sound last?

What changes if you close your fingers around the bowl?

When does the sound vibrate the strongest or the longest?

Can you hear that the sound is made up of many different tones?

Listen to the sound until it completely fades away. Feel how silent it is now...

If you wish, you can start experimenting with other things after a while: Listen to how the sound changes if you fill the bowl with water for example, or if you place the bowl on different body parts or materials. How does the sound change in different places – in large/small rooms, outside, under trees, near water, on stones?

What happens when you hit the bowl with different mallets?

Can you keep the sound flowing "endlessly" by running the mallet around the rim of the bowl with gentle but constant pressure? The sound will then become very intense, and with a little practice you can feel how everything around and within you will start to vibrate.

Let your imagination run free and follow the sound.

# Dolphin Breathing

Dolphins have fascinated humans since the beginning of time. There are many stories and legends about their connection to humans. They send out a feeling of playful ease and spirited zest for life that draws us in like magic. Just like humans, dolphins breathe air. Since they live in the water, they have to come to the surface to breathe. Dolphins breathe in deeply, hold their breath while they are under water and then breathe out like an explosion when they come back to the surface. When they breathe in, they exchange most of the air in their lungs and thus get a high dose of oxygen. We humans exchange only a little amount of our breathing air per breath. Many think that dolphins have a higher consciousness compared to humans due to this special way of breathing. Dolphins can hold their breath under water for a long time depending on the type of dolphin, from seven minutes to an hour!

While dolphins have kept a strong connection to the air, we humans often feel strongly drawn to the water. Our cells consist mainly of water and our tears have almost the same salt content and composition of seawater. I am convinced that we can learn more about ourselves and life itself if we learn more about the way that dolphins breathe. Dolphin breathing certainly helps us to feel more awake, clearer and happier. Since breathing is important for supplying our brains with oxygen, the following breathing experiments should be done outside in the fresh air (or at least with the windows wide open).

### Dolphin Breathing 1

Get comfortable so that your breath can flow freely. Breathe in deeply through your nose, count quietly in your head to four and hold your breath for four more seconds. Breathe out in one strong breath with your mouth slightly open as though you are blowing out forty candles on a birthday cake.

Repeat this breathing pattern in sets of four for as long as it feels good.

This breathing rhythm is very helpful when you are stressed, tense, anxious, scared, angry or the like. I often use it when I am out and about, have to wait, or when I have to take in and remember a lot of information (so it is good for any type of learning!). I also use it when I need to relax or free myself from bad feelings. You will quickly see how free and clear you will feel and what a good mood you will be in.

### Dolphin Breathing 2[1]

Find a place where you won't be disturbed and get comfortable. When you are ready, observe your breathing for a while; the way it flows in and out of you. Just breathe, you don't have to do anything, just observe...

After a while, you can start to imagine that there is a blowhole, just like a dolphin's, in the middle of the top of your head. Can you feel it? When you breathe in, it opens wide.

You are breathing lightly and easily through the blowhole.

---

[1] Inspiration: *Iruka No Kokyo*, by James Deacon

Feel how the energy flows into you. It flows through your head into your lungs and gives your body new energy and strength. When you breathe out, everything that is not good for you bursts out like a water fountain from your blowhole. Your entire body unloads and is freed of all burdens. Then, fresh, pleasant energy flows into your body again each time you breathe in through the blowhole in your head.

Breathe through your blowhole as long as you can and as long as you want to! This way, you give your body not only oxygen, but also cosmic life energy so that you feel strong and balanced.

If you want to, you can also use the counting pattern from above with this breathing experiment and see if it feels good.

# Walking Meditation

You can do this meditation wherever you are: inside or outside, on the street, in the forest, even when you are climbing stairs – any place where you can walk and take steps. In the beginning, however, it may be easiest for you if you choose a place where you can concentrate completely on yourself.

Start by walking forward at a normal pace. Keep yourself straight and upright, but at the same time relaxed. Look forward without really looking at anything. Just let yourself go.

Now you can start walking slower and slower. At one point you may become a bit unstable and your steps may be wobbly and uncertain. If this happens, walk a little faster again until you find a steady rhythm and feel free and good.

Observe your body. Does your breathing flow lightly and evenly? Is it deep or shallow?

Can you feel how your heels touch the ground and then slowly roll off the tips of your toes?

Feel the weight of your body on your feet...

Is it evenly spread throughout the entire sole of your foot? Or do you walk more on the outside or inside of your feet?

How do your knees move?

Do you feel how your hips sway slowly from side to side?

How does your back feel? Your arms? Your head?

After a while, you will start to realize that you are walking with a quiet, flowing balance. Your steps flow lightly and relaxed, like your breathing.

When you are ready, slowly let your movements come to a stop. Stand in a relaxed position with your weight on both feet. Feel how it is different from moving...

With more and more practice, you will probably be able to walk slower and slower and with quiet strength. If you want to, you can then start trying out other things. For instance, you can match your breathing rhythm with your steps: breathe in one step, out one step. If you succeed at this, you can raise the number of steps per breath: breathe in 2-3-4 steps, breathe out 2-3-4 steps.

You can also try out other body positions. What happens, for instance, if you lightly move your head, tilt it forward or sideways, move it in circles, stretch your arms out in front of you, hold your breath, suck in your stomach and so on?

After some practice, this meditation can help you to quickly and easily find your balance and strength. You can do it anywhere, anytime, and especially when you feel unhappy, stressed, impatient, angry and unbalanced.

# Whirlwind

The whirlwind spinning meditation is fun and you have probably already done it before anyway!

Spread your arms out at your sides like wings and start spinning. You should spin with the Earth, from west to east: if you are in the northern hemisphere, you would turn counter clockwise, if you are in the southern hemisphere, you would turn clockwise. You can start slowly and then go faster and faster. What's important is that you don't lose your balance and fall down, but instead, find your own spinning rhythm so you feel like you could spin "forever."

Try to keep your feet turning in a small circle and let your breath flow as slowly as possible. And now spin and dance until you feel fresh and "energized" and you want to come to a stop...

If you get dizzy, here is a helpful tip: stop, lay the palms of your hands together in front of your face, like you are praying and look only at your thumbs.

Everything within and outside of us spins around since everything is made up of tiny little vibrating particles that dance around themselves; sometimes closer and sometimes farther apart. This form of meditation gets everything inside us vibrating and strengthens the already present spinning movement within us. That is why it is especially good when you are tired and feeling listless, but also when you are sad, depressed, or helpless. Used carefully, this exercise can also help you to activate your inner healing powers. If you are sick, however, you should listen even more closely to the signals your body gives you. They will tell you what is GOOD for you! Listen to your body and please stop immediately if something hurts, if you are dizzy or if it just does not feel right.

# Rocking

Sit comfortably on the floor with your back straight. When you are ready, hold your left nostril shut with your finger and breathe in deeply through your right nostril. Then close the right nostril and breathe out through your left nostril. Leave your finger on your right nostril and breathe in through your left nostril, and then move your finger and breathe out through your right nostril. Your finger can stay on your left nostril while you breathe in through your right nostril, move your finger again and hold your right nostril closed while you breathe out through your left nostril. Breathe in again through your left nostril, then close the left and breathe out again through the right. Breathe in through the right, move your finger, breathe out left. Breathe in left, move your finger, breathe out right. And again, breathe in right, move your finger, breathe out left, and so on.

Repeat this breathing rhythm about ten times or as long as it is fun for you.

Once you have mastered this alternating breathing method, you can start slowly rocking your upper body back and forth. Do not lean too far forward or backward, but instead settle into a soft rocking motion, taking two seconds for each movement. Repeat this a few times – you will feel how long is right for you.

Then rock your upper body side to side in the same rhythm. Softly swing side to side a few times before rocking back and forth again. Continue as long as it feels good and is fun for you, while breathing as described above.

Rocking the upper body in the form of a cross has been used for centuries by wisdom seekers to connect to the source of wisdom and life force. It helps you to recognize the things in life that really matter and to lead a happy, healthy life.

Some people also let their heads roll in circles. When you have found your own rocking rhythm and feel good with it, you can experiment with moving your head in circles, if you want and see how it affects you.

# The Magic Eye

Fill a bowl with water and place it about fifty centimeters in front of you. Lay a colored dot (for instance a piece of paper confetti) on the surface of the water. Look at the dot and focus on it WITHOUT blinking. When your eyes start to water, squint a little. The tearing will stop.

After a while, you will probably start to see other things next to the dot; things that seem to appear "out of nowhere." Keep concentrating on the dot! The exercise is over when you have to blink.

In the beginning, you may only be able to stare for a short time without blinking. Give yourself time and keep trying again and again. Indian yogis sometimes can stare without blinking for hours and can see fine energy vibrations and things that are not normally visible to the naked eye.

# Energy Journey

Find a nice object from nature: a stone or crystal, a shell, a piece of wood – whatever attracts you and speaks to you. This object will be your guide for this energy journey. Stay as long as you want on your body's individual points of energy.

Get comfortable; it is best if you lie down. If you want to, close your eyes.

Place your special guide between your legs. Let your breath flow slowly and deeply in and out. Imagine a glowing red wheel of light where your guide is lying. It is turning clockwise. When you breathe in, red light flows into the wheel... when you breathe out, red light flows out of the wheel along your legs into the ground... red light in... and out, into the ground... see how the gleaming red of the wheel glows...

When you are ready, place your guide on your stomach, about a hand's width below your belly button. Breathe deep into your stomach. Now imagine a turning wheel of orange light where your guide is. Like a carrousel, it spins around and shines in a warm orange color. When you breathe in, orange light flows from the wheel into your body, when you breathe out, you let the orange light flow back out. It flushes everything out of you that you don't need or want. Breathe in orange light... breathe out orange light...

When you are ready, you can now place your guide on your belly button. Imagine a wheel of golden light there that radiates merrily dancing sparks as it turns. When you breathe in, you ignite a golden, glowing light in your stomach, when you breathe out you burn off everything that isn't good for you in the yellow beacon of fire. Yellow in... yellow out...

When you are ready, lay your guide on the next station; on your breastbone at heart-level. Now imagine a wheel that radiates a life-giving green light. When you breathe in, draw the pleasant green light deep into you and when you breathe out let everything that you do not need blow out of you on the breeze of green light. Do you see how the green wheel of light turns evenly and powerfully in a circle?

When you are ready, you can lay your guide in the little hollow between your collar bone and your neck. Imagine a glowing wheel of blue light. Breathe in and out deeply and let the blue light flow into you when you breathe in. When you breathe out, the blue light takes away everything that weighs on you and cleanses you through and through.

When you are ready, place your guide between your eyebrows; some people call this point the third eye. Imagine a blue-violet wheel of light that shines through your whole head. Breathe the quiet blue-violet in deeply. Feel how the blue flame cleanses your entire being and when you breathe out, let everything that you do not want flow out of you.

When you are ready, lay your guide now on the middle of the top of your head. This is a very sensitive place and may still be open on small babies in the first months of their lives. Imagine a spinning wheel of light whose rays spread out like a giant umbrella over your head. In the middle of the wheel, there is a glowing violet light that pours out over you in all the colors of the rainbow. Breathe this vibrant arc of light deep into you. Let it flow over you with your breath, like a warm comforting shower. In... and out... The light shines around you and through you. Breathe deeply and evenly...

You can now take your guide in your hand and imagine that glowing white moonlight is entering the highest point of your head from above flowing through the center of the spinning wheels of light before it flows into Mother Earth. See how all the wheels of light with their different colors turn within you and your whole being is flooded with glittering white light...

Give yourself time and, at your own pace, come back to the outside world.

# Fantasy Journeys

# The Inner Dolphin

You are sitting on a boulder and looking down on the bay. The waves sparkle like a thousand diamonds. You hear their soft crashing as they roll onto the beach.

Far out in sea, you discover a small group of jumping dolphins. They play, happy and frolicking, jumping high in the air and with an elegant twist, they fall back into the water. The spray of water drops paints glittering crystal pictures in the sunlight.

How wonderful it would be to romp with them in the waves...

The dolphins notice you and come closer. Curious, they swim around you. Soon, they accept you into their group and you feel as though you are one of them.

The dolphins take you on a journey. You hold tight to one of the dolphin's back fins. Easily and quickly, you are pulled through the waves. You feel completely safe and secure; free and light.

Suddenly, the dolphins are moving slower. Astonished, you see an island rising up before you with large, green-fanned palm trees. In the middle of the island is a magnificent, gleaming golden temple.

You run towards it and allow yourself to be guided by the light. A chorus of many brilliantly ringing little bells sound an enchanting melody and from within the temple flows a warm, rainbow-colored light.

Inside the temple, there is a big round room. In the middle of the room stands a brightly glowing crystal, almost as big as you. Slowly, you step closer.

"Touch the crystal. It will give you strength and energy," you suddenly hear a voice say.

A wave of warmth and power floods through your body as you lay your hand on the stone.

"Now go to the magic spiral," you hear the voice say. "If you stand in the center of it, everything within you will be transformed into peace and lightness."

Behind the crystal glows a shimmering blue light. The fine, tube-like lines of the spiral seem to vibrate lightly. You step into the middle. As gently as a summer rain, the blue light flows from your feet, up your back, to the top of your head. It cleanses you completely and fills you with peace and quiet.

*Free* and *calm,* you look around the room. On a silk cushion by the wall sits a glowing being of light that you have only now just noticed. It beckons you with a wave and offers you a ball of light. It is light and translucent.

"Pass the ball in a circle around your whole body," says the being of light.

With the ball of light in your hands, you pass it around your body and a fine, silver net of glowing beams of light forms around you until you are completely enveloped by a cloak of light.

"The cloak of light will protect you from everything that is not good for you," explains the being of light. "Stay as long as you like. Whenever you need to fill yourself with new power and you want to find peace and quiet, you are welcome here."

*Refreshed* and *renewed,* you say your goodbyes and return to the dolphins. They carry you back, safely and quickly, through the waves, to your place in the sun on the boulder.

# The Butterfly Woman

You are walking across a meadow. Soft blades of grass gently tickle the soles of your feet, the smooth buzzing of the bees and beetles fills the air and you feel the warm sunrays on your skin. It smells like warm earth and fresh strawberries.

You come to a tree. It is *big* and *strong* and its branches stretch high into the sky. Under its sturdy roots, you discover a moss-covered opening. You bend down and look inside...

It smells pleasant, fresh and mossy. You suddenly notice that you can go through the opening. Inside, it is *warm* and *peaceful*... And wonderfully silent...

After a while, your eyes get used to the darkness and you discover a wooden ladder that goes up the inside of the tree.

Where does it go?

Curious, you start to climb the rungs. The wood feels velvety and smooth on your hands and feet. It smells nice, like sap and spicy pine needles...

Far above you, you see a soft light that glows brighter and brighter with each step. The closer you come, the more the light surrounds you. The rays flow like a waterfall around your body and trickle down the tree trunk in colorful points of light.

The light is now so bright and gleaming that you have to close your eyes.

Suddenly, the ladder ends. You have arrived at a platform. A sweet, pleasant-smelling scent wafts into your nose. When you open your eyes you are looking directly into the beaming face of a beautiful woman.

"Welcome," says the woman and her voice sounds like a warm summer wind.

"Who are you?"

"I am the butterfly woman."

Only now do you notice her butterfly wings. They shimmer like colorful soap bubbles in the sunlight.

The butterfly woman looks at you with a loving smile and says, "I have a gift for you."

She points to a small hollow in the bark. In it lies a crystal ball that shimmers like a rainbow.

Gently, the woman says, "Look inside! *Now…* you will see something inside that is meant only for you... something that is good for you... that will help you... Look inside..."

"Take the images with you so that you always have them and remember them.

You can always come back to me if you need to," says the butterfly woman quietly.


Grateful, you say goodbye and climb back down the ladder.

With each step, the light becomes weaker. But you still feel the warmth and glow within you and you know that you can always come back to this place.

# Dolphin Journey

You are in a hut on the beach looking out at the water, which glistens in the sunlight and shimmers like diamonds.

Seagulls are screeching and you hear the calming sound of the waves.

You go down to the beach. The sand is warm from the sun and it gushes softly between your toes. You lie down on your back and enjoy the soft, comforting warmth of the grains of sand nestling against your body.

The clouds go by overhead... slowly... always creating new shapes.

It smells like saltwater and algae. A light wind gently caresses your body.

Suddenly, you hear a long whistle. In the ocean in front of you, you see a fin sticking out of the water. Close to the beach, the fin moves back and forth in a smooth and flowing motion – and you keep hearing the whistle again and again. It sounds like a call.

You walk into the water. It feels pleasant and refreshing as it gently washes around your feet. The fin belongs to a dolphin. Is he calling you?

As you move closer, he floats calmly in the water and seems to smile at you.

Now you are so close that you can almost touch him. His dark eyes look deep into you, filled with love.

The dolphin swims toward you and you feel his smooth skin on your legs as he glides softly by you. He swims around you once then floats next to you on the surface of the water and you can touch his back fin. Trustingly, you hold on tight. His fin feels soft and silky.

The dolphin lets out a joyful sound. Slowly, he begins to move and together you glide gently and safely like the waves through the water.

You feel the dolphin's *strength* and vitality in your body. You feel the *joy* and *cheer* that he feels from the speed. Like an arrow you shoot through the water together.

Then the dolphin starts to dive into the water with you.

The ocean is infinite. You seem to be flying through the water. *Free* and *happy*.

Suddenly a large rock appears before you. Algae, sea grass and corals gently sway back and forth. Colorful fish drift in the waves and little seahorses dance joyfully in the water.

The dolphin swims with you to an opening in the rock and you hear a wonderful melody. It leads you to a bright, glowing place where a group of playing dolphins frolic carefree and joyously.

It is fun to watch them; to feel their joy. They invite you to join them and play with them…

When you have had enough, you separate from the group. The dolphins wave to you with their flippers and accompany you and your dolphin for a while as you swim out of the rock cave and back out into the open sea.

With even motions, you glide through the water back to the beach.

You say goodbye to your dolphin friend. He answers you with a long whistle and you know that he will always take you on a journey whenever you want to.

# At the End of the Rainbow

You are sitting at the window and looking outside. It has rained and the air is clear and fresh. On the horizon, you see a rainbow appear: first blue, then green, yellow, orange, red – the colors melt together and stretch across the sky in a beautiful, soft arc.

Then you suddenly hear a soft voice: "Do you want to fly to the rainbow with me?"

A small bird is sitting on the windowsill right near you. Did the voice come from him?

"Yes," you hear in reply to your silent question. And while you are still wondering how you could possibly fly on such a small bird, you realize that the bird is getting bigger and bigger. Soon he is the same size as you and you can comfortably grab hold of his silky feathers and swing up onto his back.

The little bird lifts off into the air and glides up into the clouds. His wings flutter smoothly and quietly, up and down. Far below, you see the earth and everything is so tiny...

You drift higher and higher until a pink cloud appears before you. The little bird flies toward it and lands. He carefully sets you down and your feet touch the cloud. It feels like velvety rabbit fur.

"Where are we?" you ask.

"At the end of the rainbow," your feathered friend says.

Then you discover the colorful glowing rays that arch across the sky. The pink ray leads to your cloud. Many other clouds float next to you, each one a different color.

In the middle of the clouds, you see a very special cloud. It glows with a golden shine, spraying bright sparks as though it is raining little glittering stars.

"This is the golden source of life," says the little bird. "This is where you will find whatever you are looking for."

"What do you mean?" you ask.

"You will find comfort here...

You will find counsel here...

You will find peace here...

You will find courage and confidence here...

You will find warmth and security here...

You will find light here...

You will find tranquility here...

You will find trust here...

You will find love here...

Every spark of light that springs from this source is a gift to everything that is alive," continues the little bird. "If you want, I will take you there. If you catch one of the golden sparks, you can make a wish!"

The little bird flies you to the source of life. The closer you come, the brighter and more radiant the golden light becomes. You feel the warmth and the bubbling spirit of the fountains of light that gush from the middle of the source like a geyser.

You reach out your hand and try to grasp one of the sparks. The dancing flashes are not easy to catch…

But then you simply open your fingers and hold your hand in the air. Suddenly, a tiny, bright, glowing, golden spark lands on your hand. It feels nice and tingly and at the same time very delicate.

"Place your hand on your heart and if you have a question or a wish, you can think of it *now* and you will receive an answer," says the little bird.

As if in a dream, you float through the sea of glittering colorful clouds. You turn around one last time and you see the golden fireworks in the middle of the clouds.

Peacefully, you cuddle in the bird's soft feathers and let him carry you... until he softly sets you back down on the windowsill.

"Thank you," you say and bid him farewell.

"You can always call me in your thoughts when you need me. Then we will fly to the golden source at the end of the rainbow," says the little bird before he flies away.

# "I Am in My Element"

In this section, you can find out which element you feel most comfortable with. We all have different preferences and tendencies. Some people are airy; they fly from one experience to the next. Some are as solid as a rock in their opinions or deeply rooted in the earth. Some are fiery and explosive, some are unmoving and constant and as solid as a rock in the shifting surf of life. Our language reflects these aspects. Naturally, we usually have more than one of these aspects in us. But there is often one element that we feel most attracted to. If you know your element, you can use this knowledge in many situations in your life. You will get to know your strengths and weaknesses better and find out which element helps you the most and can heal you, and how you can keep your inner balance. You will find examples of how to do this with each element. Have fun discovering your element!

# Air

You are standing on a rock high up in the mountains. The clear blue sky above you seems close enough to touch. Your gaze drifts across the snow-capped mountaintops, down into the green valleys and out to the glittering turquoise ocean in the distance. A refreshing south wind blows through your hair. It carries the spicy scent of mountain thyme. You breathe deeply and take in the cooling, snowy air. A huge bird circles above you. With outstretched wings, it glides through the air. It flaps its wings a few times and is guided into the wind current. It is carried with almost no movement, as fast as an arrow, until it slowly and powerfully flaps its wings again and soars up along the mountainside. The bird plays with the wind and the wind plays with it. They dance together…

You spread your arms out and slowly spin like a top. The wind dances around you and suddenly you feel it softly lifting your body… You can fly!

It blows you softly and cheerfully up into the vastness of the sky. It carries you and you feel free and light as you float through the air like a bird. You sense how you can flow with the movement of the wind, simply gliding in the currents. Sometimes you are being carried effortlessly, drifting like a leaf in the wind. Sometimes you flap your arms powerfully but quietly to fly back into the wind current…

Up and down, back and forth. The wind shows you distant lands, new, unfamiliar scents and exotic smells; animals that you have only seen in books... It tells you stories of its adventures and its travels around the world. It takes you to isolated dales where wild horses run free and graze in lush, green meadows. It sweeps you far out over deep blue ocean waves that are so high that even tanker ships seem small and meaningless.

You are one with the wind; you dance with it and it with you – just like it dances with the bird, the waves and the leaves. Animals, plants, everything that lives is connected through the breath of wind. You breathe the same air as your family, your friends, who may live in other countries; the elephant in Africa, the tiger in India or the whale in the vast ocean.

You are free like the wind. You can blow into any nook and cranny and let your thoughts flow free. Who can hold or lock up the wind! Fly and dance with the wind like a bird. Breathe the wind and let yourself be carried, free and without boundaries...

When you are ready, come back to the outer world. Take the feeling of unlimited freedom and lightness with you.

## Do You Belong to the Air Family?

Do you like to do a lot of different things? Do you like to try new things? Do you experiment and let yourself flow from one experience to the next like a butterfly that flutters from flower to flower? Maybe you love the changes in every life situations: your moods change from shouting for joy to deep sorrow as do your preferences for clothing and colors, projects and interests, sometimes even for friends. Are you easily inspired and swept along if something sounds interesting and exciting and promises adventure and fun?

Members of the air family generally like to travel and curiously explore the unknown and uncharted. Like the wind, they can blow into every crack, but never remain in one place for very long.

Are you always having new ideas and sudden flashes of insight? When your environment asks about your current project, have you already long since moved on to the next one?

Air dancers like to follow their spontaneous ideas and like to play with everything and everyone. They don't like to be tied down. Like the wind, they can be very changeable and take on many forms, from a soft spring breeze to a thunderous whirlwind. Like a joyful fall wind that wantonly blows the hats off people's heads they are very playful and love to joke.

## The Language of the Air

The wind can teach us many special things, even if we do not belong to the air family. It shows us, for instance, that it is sometimes important to let go and be flexible like bamboo. When the wind blows strong and head-on, such as when you are having problems, when it feels as though you are constantly struggling against a headwind, it often helps if you don't resist it. It takes a lot of strength and energy to resist things that cannot be changed or influenced by you. The wind will blow, sometimes softly, sometimes powerfully. Have you ever tried to "lean into the wind" in a storm and let yourself be carried? If you let yourself be carried, you can ride its energy. Instead of it blowing in your face and the cold air taking your breath away, it lends you its strength and supports you.

The birds, our relatives in the sky, know the language and secrets of the wind like no other creature on earth. When they set out on their long journey to the warmer climates on the other side of the globe, the wind is their loyal companion. Without its help, they would not be able to overcome the long distances. They know how to let the wind carry them and let themselves drift so they can sail through the air on the wind's strength.

Dance in the wind like a bamboo reed, light and flexible. Watch the boughs of a tree that rock back and forth in a storm. They follow the movement of the wind so their branches do not snap and break, yet they are firmly connected to the trunk and Mother Earth. Connect with your inner source of power. Then you can dance through even the strongest storms in your life without breaking or being blown over.

Dance with the wind and listen to its stories and it will share its wisdom and ideas with you.


### Balance for Air Dancers

If you are a child of the air and like the breezy sides of life, it may be that you sometimes need some balance so you do not "lift off" and lose your inner balance. Otherwise, you may flutter from one idea to the next but never put your good ideas into action.

It is, therefore, good for air people to be in contact with the earth. You can, for instance, lie down on the warm floor of the forest or in a meadow or plant something. You can plant seeds in flowerpots on the balcony or windowsill, plant trees in a city park or take part in planting projects offered by environmental conservation groups, schools and other institutions. You can ask friends and family if they can give you access to a piece of land where you can set up a little garden or a "magic forest" – maybe even ask your friends to do it with you. It is a lot of fun to plan a project like this and watch it grow. Whenever you feel tense or stressed, these activities will balance you out and help restore your inner harmony.

The element water can also have a balancing effect on you. A warm bath – perhaps there is even a hot spring somewhere nearby – can sometimes work wonders. If you live near a lake, the ocean or a stream, the steady sound of the waves and surf or flowing water can help you find inner calm and clarity.

If you like, you can try the drum journey in the first chapter (rhythm meditation, page 6). You can play in harmony with the heartbeat of Mother Earth if you need strength and energy or want to cope with a project, work or a challenging situation.

In addition, or if you do not have the time or ability to plant something, drum or take a bath, you can get a bottle of pure eucalyptus oil. The smell of eucalyptus brings children of the air "down to earth" and helps them find their inner balance. You can either dab the oil directly onto your body (careful: not too much or it may burn), for instance on your temples or wrists or on your clothes, or burn it in a fragrance lamp.

# Water

You are in a lush, jungle-like forest. Long, light-green lichens hang from the trees and weave a magical curtain. Above you, silver-green fronds stretch out to make a roof. The air is warm and pleasant. Birds sing their melodies and whistle in their various languages. Sunbeams paint dancing patterns on the narrow path before you. You hear the quiet whispering of the wind in the soft, green leaves. From within a hollow tree trunk, a little chipmunk observes you. It makes funny little noises and twitches the tip of its bushy red-brown tail with interest. A few shells from the nuts it has eaten are scattered around the tree trunk.

The path winds beneath the leafy canopy through which the light shines and shimmers in beautiful turtle-shell patches, and leads down into a little ravine. A crystal clear stream gushes white foam over rounded boulders. The water surface glitters in the sun like liquid silver. The water drops rush by you, babbling and bouncing joyfully. Where do they come from?

You decide to climb over the rocks and up the stream. The first step is ice-cold, but the fast current and little air bubbles softly massage your feet and legs and soon you do not feel the cold anymore. It is fun to hop from stone to stone. The stones are warm from the sun; some are covered in soft moss, others washed with clear water. You find your path, stepping further and further up the stream...

Suddenly, you hear a steady roar. It gets louder and louder

until you round a bend and two giant boulders appear before you. The water winds its way, trickling in larger and smaller rivulets over and through the stones. You climb up on one of the boulders and look directly down into a round stone basin; from above, a curtain of white, glittering water drops falls down into it.

The water in the basin is crystal clear and shimmers green-blue. You can see the boulders that form the floor of the pool far below. In the middle, the water is churning and whirling from the falling drops; it is foamy from all the air bubbles. An opaque veil of water drops floats in the air and drapes itself over you, cool and soft, on your skin. The sunrays conjure a glowing rainbow on the white curtain before you.

You sit down on a soft, sun-warmed patch of moss and watch the bubbling, swirling water funnel in the middle of the basin: a flow that never stops...

You feel the strength of the water within you: a gentle, powerful energy. White, foamy energy that finds its own way, even when boulders and other obstacles try to stand in its way. Constant and with a steady flow, the water finds its path, washes around stones and giant trees, flows through tiny cracks and openings and is strong enough to carry tree trunks and ships. It connects distant lands and the cells in our body...

You are the water; the water is a part of you. You are the waterfall.

Feel how the water flows into you from above, flows through you and connects you with everything that exists. You are one with the water. Let yourself just flow and be carried...

Feel the strength that flows within you... the power that is you...

Feel how strong you are, how connected to everything.

Feel how the current of the water flows eternally. A never-ending cycle of giving and receiving – forever flowing...

When you are ready, slowly come back into your body. Take the feeling of flowing and being connected with you and return to your pool of strength whenever you want to.

## Do You Belong to the Water Family?

Water people splash playfully and joyfully through life like a clear mountain stream. They are open and curious and love the company of others. If you belong to the water family, you may like to help other beings, regardless of whether they are humans, animals or plants. You are able to easily empathize and soothe or comfort others.

Like the water, water children like to flow around obstacles and problems. They love harmony and prefer to avoid direct conflict. They are very inventive and imaginative and are strongly tied to the Moon and her energies. Like air children, water children do not like to be tied down or to have their fantasies blocked. They have to flow freely, otherwise their energies become dammed up like a reservoir and when pent-up energies then suddenly burst free, they can easily break things…

Water children often have healing abilities, whether they simply listen or give advice or, for instance, let healing energy flow through their hands.


## The Language of Water

Water is life. When we listen to the many voices with which water speaks, the splashing of a stream, the steady rush of the waves on the beach, the drumming of the rain on a window, the roar of a waterfall, we discover a lot about the flow of life! Have you ever looked down into a deep ravine where far below a clear stream happily jumps over the rocks? Many, many drops of water, constantly and merrily hopping down the mountains to the ocean, have carved deep valleys over the course of time. They show us that we can achieve more with a soft, constant strength than with pure physical strength and force. When we are connected to everything that surrounds us, we can achieve so much. Many, many drops of water together have the power to wash away giant boulders on the beach and turn them into grains of sand. You can also achieve many things if you combine your strength with the strength of others. Together you are strong, and sometimes you can let yourself be carried or sometimes carry others.

You can learn from the water to trust that your course will always continue to flow and move forward, no matter how easy or difficult things may seem. You are a part of the river of life, even if you come across a stone that seems to block your way. We are all part of the great circle of life on earth, like the drops of water that fall from the clouds to the ground and begin their journey to the sea and from there someday change their form again when the sun sends them back to the sky and they begin their cycle anew... Your journey in life flows the same way, always continuing on, and it is up to you to decide if the stones in your path will block you or if you choose to flow around them.

Listen to the soothing rolling of the waves or the steady murmur of a stream when you need comfort. Let yourself drift and be carried in shallow, warm water. Wash away everything that troubles you and let the water carry it away and cleanse you… The water will calm, balance and heal you. It will give you courage and advice and steer you back into the flow of life.

## Balance for Water Bearers

If you are a water child, your desire to be in harmony with others may be so strong that your own boundaries melt away and you lose sight of your own needs. Many water children must, therefore, learn to set boundaries and distinguish themselves in order to show their uniqueness to the world. Water children often seem to have a tendency to melt into their emotions or be "washed away" and overcome by their feelings. Therefore, it is important for them to channel their flow into a tangible form once in a while. Maybe you like to paint, or play music or do handcrafts, such as pottery, toning, making mosaics, carving, or sculpting. All of these forms of expression allow you to combine your flowing, creative energy with physical activity and design. Let your thoughts and ideas flow freely and at the same time, form them into something tangible and grounded.

Maybe you like to dance and move to music. Dancing allows water people to let their movements flow and express their feelings without losing themselves: Your body constantly reminds you of your own form and possibilities and lets you find your own rhythm and way of moving.

It is very important, however, that you learn to recognize and know your limits, both within you and outside of yourself; and at the same time, let your inner energy flow freely. Otherwise, it may get clogged and become destructive. If you have the feeling that a wave of emotions is washing over you and threatening to knock you over, just let it flow out onto the beach of your creativity and calm down; paint, play music, dance, take a walk, whatever you feel like doing! You will find that it will help you.

# Fire

It is a balmy, mild summer evening. The sand beneath your feet is still pleasantly warm from the day's sunshine. A final orange glow blazes on the horizon before you. Then, only the red, pink and golden glowing clouds remind you of the strength of the sun. The crickets begin their steady evening chirping song. A jasmine bush with its white and blushing pink petals fills the air with a honey-sweet scent.

Dusk sets in and the night slowly comes, enveloping everything in a blue-black velvet cloak, stitched with thousands of glittering stars. You see the bright path of the Milky Way shining above you and the strikingly bright star up there is Sirius...

Suddenly, the spicy smell of wood smoke drifts across your nose and in the distance you see the flickering light of a fire dancing on the trunks of the trees. You walk toward it and come to a clearing. In the middle of it you see a frolicking fire. The boughs and branches have been carefully stacked to form a tepee. In the center, where the fire burns the hottest, you see the white, glowing, pulsating heat. Flames, in shades of orange, flow upward like waves over the thicker branches of the wooden tepee, before they flicker, dark yellow-orange, free and unbound into the sky. You hear the fire crackle and sizzle. Sometimes it buzzes and hisses when it touches sappy pieces of wood. The flame fairies dance and celebrate cheerfully. They know their powerful energy can transform everything. A spray of sparks suddenly bursts into the air as a large branch groans and sinks into the flames. The wave of hot air sets your face aglow for a brief moment.

Look into the dancing flames...

If you want to, throw everything that saddens or scares you, makes you feel guilty or sick, everything that you do not like into the fire *now*...

Surrender everything to the flame fairies so that they can transform it into smoke and fine ash, just like the wood, until there is nothing left of its original form. Imagine how the flames gather up your worries, your guilt, and the things that scare you or make you sick and dissolve them in their heat. They are powerful wizards who can transform anything.

The flames are a part of you; you are a part of them. Feel the embers within you...

Feel the cleansing and healing power...

When you are ready, come back to the outer world. Feel how the power of the fire has cleansed you and set you free.

## Do You Belong to the Fire Family?

Have you ever heard the saying, "playing with fire?" People who play with fire love adventure and generally do not ever shy away from risk if a particular undertaking seems interesting. They trust in their strengths and are convinced that they can transform things with their powers. Are you overflowing with ideas and good at organizing, planning and putting them into action? Perhaps you can inspire others and sweep them along so that they join you and burn with interest in your project just like you.

Fire children like to experiment and play with a vast variety of things. They love to improve and transform their environment. Building, decorating, parties, school events, organizing and participating in theater and dance performances, playing in bands and orchestras; these are all areas that may interest fiery folk. They do not necessarily have to be in the spotlight, but their glowing enthusiasm and their burning drive often put them in a position of leadership, simply because others do not muster nearly as much energy.

Sometimes, however, their enthusiasm evaporates quickly, like a straw fire that burns fast and bright and then goes out. Their interest has to be ignited again and again by something new, appealing and beautiful and then held. If there is no wood or other material to burn, the fire goes out.

Fire people are very open to all things beautiful, whether natural or artificial. They surround and adorn themselves with beautiful things and decorate their environment. They also usually like the heat. They enjoy sunbathing; warm, fiery colors and sounds brighten their mood.

Fire people generally see things clearly and are very observant. However, sometimes your friends may not be very understanding when you speak your mind or voice your opinions directly; instead they feel hurt or offended. As a child of fire, you see where changes need to be made and do not hesitate to say it. But your environment is not always ready or willing to accept your advice, no matter how well-meaning it may be.


## The Language of Fire

Have you ever built a fire? First paper, then straw, dry reeds or other easily flammable material, then carefully laid out dry wood and, finally, lit it? Have you ever seen the different shades in the flames; yellow to dark orange at the tips and white hot in the center where it is the hottest? Fire has many faces. When we are open to it, we can learn a lot about transformation and contrasts from it. Fire provides us with heat, but its heat can also be destructive. It cooks our food and makes rice and potatoes edible, but it can also burn down entire fields of grain and forests with its power. Fire transforms wood into fine ash, hard metal into glowing red liquid, and ice into water. Fire is part of our lives, part of the Earth: We live on a thin, cooled crust of our planet under which hot, molten layers seethe all the way to the Earth's core.

If we learn to understand the language of fire, we can better understand the transformation of energy in our lives. We learn to handle intense energies which we express in the form of intense emotions, for instance, when we are in love, angry, desperate or inspired so that they will nourish us and move us forward instead of damaging and burning us. We learn not to go up in flames, but instead to guide our flame so it gives us warmth, inspiration and drive and nourishes us.

Observe the fire in its different forms and you will learn to distinguish how you can best maintain your fire. Discover the fire within you and explore what ignites it, what makes it flare up or go out.

## Balance for Fire Salamanders

If you are a fire person, it helps to find out how you can feed your fire and maintain it without "burning yourself out" or burning others. Your fiery zeal, your fiery ideas and your enthusiasm are important. It can be helpful to get to know the characteristics of your fire so that you can harness it and it can warm and nourish you and others. Explore which materials help your fire burn steadily and with the most power. Physical activities such as Aikido or other martial arts, archery, rock-climbing, flamenco dancing, and Qi Gong are only a few of the things that you can try out. Perhaps it would be fun for you to play in a band or orchestra? Perhaps you are especially drawn to percussion instruments? Drumming is good for finding your own rhythm and letting off steam. The whirlwind meditation exercise in the first chapter can also help you get to know your fire being better.

Go outside into the forest or on a beach when you feel burned out, but also when your fire is burning too wild and threatening to burn everything. Listen to the wind singing in the leaves or the waves crashing on the beach. If this is not an option, you can also burn sandalwood in a fragrance lamp. If you have a rose quartz or yellow citrine you can move it in circles over your stomach or just lay the stone on your stomach.

All of these things can guide you to a better understanding of your fire and lead you to your balance and inner strength.

# Earth

You are climbing a windy path up a mountain. The rocks beneath your hands and feet are warm from the sun and covered with lichens. The air is fresh and rich and a light west wind blows softly across your face. Little flowers glow in bright colors on the bare, velvety brown alpine meadow next to the path. You feel the power of Mother Earth that allows them to grow despite the altitude up here in the mountains.

After a while, you come to a plateau. Steep rock cliffs loom above you. You discover a narrow opening, barely visible between two ledges. The opening is just big enough for you to slip into. Within, everything seems dark and black. You hear the echo of your steps and realize the cave is very big. It is warm and smells pleasant – like sweetgrass and sage. You sit and wait until your eyes adjust to the darkness. You run your hands along the smooth rocks next to you and beneath you. It seems as though the stone has been smoothed and polished.

Suddenly, a weak light shines in the darkness. You can just barely make out a tunnel that leads to the light. Carefully, you feel your way forward using your feet to find the path. The scent of sweetgrass and the light grow stronger and stronger. The tunnel leads you to a large underground cavern; a warm fire is burning in the middle. On the walls and ceiling, thousands of gemstones glitter in the flickering light of the flames in all of the colors of the rainbow. Next to the fire, you see a small basin with steam rising from it. A spring, warmed from the heat of the Earth's core, gushes up between the rocks. It is wonderfully warm and comfortable in the cave.

You climb into the hotspring. The water gushes around you, comforting and massaging you as it softly bubbles around your body. You feel completely secure and protected. The yellow-orange light of the fire flows over the crystal walls of the cave and surrounds you with a gentle cloak of rays. Deep and steady, you feel the heartbeat of Mother Earth... It pulses comfortingly and flows into you through the waves of the water.

You are safe and secure here. Feel how your body, your whole being, becomes quiet, at one with Mother Earth...

Feel how your body, your whole being, is flooded with light and cleansed by the glow of the fire and the crystals... Warmth and peace and light envelop you and heal you...

Stay here as long as you like. Enjoy the peace, warmth, safety and comfort in Mother Earth's lap.

When you are ready, you can get out of the hotspring and slowly go back, out of the cave. This is your secret place and you can come back here whenever you need to.

## Do You Belong to the Earth Family?

As an earth child, you probably love the quiet and a comfortable home. Perhaps you like to cuddle in your pillows and read or daydream. Earth people generally vibrate slower, which means they need time and quiet to make decisions and think about things. As an earth child, you are not always comfortable with spontaneous changes. Things have to have "rhyme and reason" before you are able to get involved in them.

Nourishing others, helping them, taking care of friends, the weak, sick, and underprivileged is very near to the hearts of earth children. They are often wonderful cooks and conjure delicious meals for themselves and others. They find it fun to plant their own garden and tend it. Earth children usually devote themselves to caring for pets entrusted to them. They see them as more than just playmates and take constant care of their well-being and health.

Do you have an ability to sense the atmosphere and moods and are you sensitive to fluctuations in your environment? In general, earth children are helpful and need harmony. They do not like to fight and it is important to them that everything is peaceful.

Building with clay, for instance, or handcrafts such as weaving are activities that many earth children like. They create comfortable and cozy places where others also like to spend time. Members of the earth family often are good riders; their quiet and balanced manner transfers to their four-legged friends.

As an earth child, you need a certain calmness and stability in your life. Too many changes and too much movement can quickly become too much for you to handle. When you take care of your needs, your power can unfold and you can create and inspire many beautiful, healing, and important things.

## The Language of the Earth

If you want to learn the language of the earth, you have to open your senses wide, because it is a very quiet language although it holds great power. Lie down on the warm ground on a beautiful sunny day. Close your eyes and simply wait. After a while, you will probably feel a deep, steady thumping. Your entire body may begin to vibrate with this powerful rhythm. That is the heartbeat of Mother Earth. It calms us and gives us a feeling of being nourished and cared for.

Perhaps you have noticed how different earth can smell and feel: dry, warm earth is rough and crumbly; damp, cool earth is soft, sometimes slimy and smells very different. Depending on the season and weather, the Earth has different characteristics and abilities. In the winter, the roots of the plants and seeds sleep in her lap, in the spring, she and Father Sun and the rain give many creatures life. In the warmth of the summer, life matures and blooms in abundance before the powers retreat back into her in the fall. Thus, the Earth is closely connected to the cycle of life.

If you like, you can plant your own garden. This can also be done in flower pots if no other place is available. When you study the Earth and her language, you can not only learn a lot about the cycle of life, giving and receiving, nourishing and fostering, but also about many other qualities such as reliability, trust, and dependability.

When you are well grounded, you can build your ideas on a stable foundation and put them into action. Like the seeds, they will mature and grow in the fertile ground in their yearly cycle until they reach full bloom.

The language of the earth is important for us all, otherwise our fire may go out like a straw fire, our water will run off without direction or evaporate or we will drift away on the wind like a disoriented leaf...

## Balance for Earth Spirits

Do you sometimes hesitate and sometimes go back and forth on a decision? Do you have wonderful plans and ideas, but it takes forever for you to take the first step to realize them? Earth children often sleep so deeply within the earth and are so firmly rooted that it is not easy for them to get things moving or get themselves moving. To find balance, regular and steady activities that also get you moving are good for you. Maybe you might like to use the walking meditation (see page 15) to learn how to find balance in your movement. If you like water, you can enjoy the steady movement of swimming. Take a walk or jog on the beach where you can hear the steady, constant crashing of the waves in motion. Drumming can also help you find a regularly flowing rhythm in movement. Everything that brings you into a steady flow is good for you. Pottery, building or modeling with clay, Qi Gong, riding a bike, sailing, or kayaking; all of these activities can help you to be flexible so that you do not "get stuck" or stand too firmly rooted in one position.

Your ideas and opinions are important. Therefore, allow yourself to play around, to experiment and to do things that are fun for you! Even if you have not thought everything out or planned each detail. Take the time that you need to let the seeds of your thoughts mature and then let them grow and bloom. Trust that they will go through their life cycle, nourished from your fertile ground but also from the many other good powers in this world.

# Wood

It is early in the morning, the magical hour before sunrise. You are looking out the window. The stars are still shining in the sky, but the birds are greeting the new day with their lively singing. You go outside; the fresh morning air blows gently across your face. Slowly, the sky begins to change color on the horizon; the blue-black darkness of night begins to make way for the fire of the sun that pales the stars.

The chorus of chirping birds now fills the air loud and clear. Their joy seems contagious. You follow the ever-changing spectacle of the starting day playing on the colorfully lit stage of the sky. The first rays have faintly lightened the deep blue of the sky, and the horizon glows in rich tones of orange and red. This is the hour of new beginnings and powerful meditation in which all beings prepare themselves and welcome the coming day.

Now the bright ball of the sun is glowing in the distance. The first rays transform the dewdrops on the meadow into thousands of glittering crystals. An ancient oak tree stretches her leaves toward the sun and drinks in the light. You sit down between her roots, lean your back on her wide, knotty trunk and she tells you her story...

*Warm and comfortable, the little acorn nestles in the earth under the fallen leaves. The whole winter long, it gathers its strength and sleeps beneath a thick, white blanket of snow until a warm rain shower awakens it in the spring. The first powerful rays of sun melt the snow crystals and nourish the little acorn with minerals and other nutrients. Determinedly, it stretches. Its roots dig themselves into the soft, warm earth to give it stability.*

*One day, it feels strong enough and a short, yellow-white sprout grows from its center and splits its shell in two. After a few days, it stretches its head curiously out of the ground. How beautiful and bright and warm the world is! The little acorn has many plans. Rooted firmly in the ground, it stretches its delicate but strong stem toward the sun. Light, water and the nutrients from the earth give it everything it needs to grow.*

Many seasons pass...

The young acorn grows bigger and stronger. It learns to dance with the wind and defy the weather. It learns to be supple and flexible so it won't break. Sometimes it has to change directions so that its leaves get enough sunlight and it is not overshadowed or pushed away by other trees. Firmly rooted in the ground, it keeps its balance. It adjusts to the conditions of its environment without losing sight of its goal. Its branches form an overhanging, protective roof and reach far out. Many birds and other life forms find a safe home within it.

The oak tree is big and strong. Ten children have to join hands to go around her trunk. She connects the heavens with the Earth and each year in the spring, she still bursts forth with new life...

The new, delicate green leaves of the oak tree rustle quietly above you in the morning breeze. The sun brightens the whole sky and a new day has begun. Feel the confidence and quiet strength of the oak tree within you. Grow like it grows: balanced from within your center. Feel your strength, which is eternal, even if you yield or change direction. Grow and become, strong like the oak tree, trusting your life and your inner goal.

## Do You Belong to the Wood Family?

Are you good at organizing things? Do you go forward with determination and try to put your plans into effect? Wood people are usually people of action. When they have an idea in mind, they put it into action. They are not easily thrown off balance. Wood people know what they want and work unerringly toward their goals. At the same time, they are open to many things and can adjust to change if necessary.

Members of the wood family usually have a clear picture of their future. They see the big picture and can thus plan their actions wisely and in advance. With their clear and dynamic nature, they are important sources of inspiration and good orientation points for their environments. If, however, their drive to grow and explore is hindered too strongly, wood people can react very angrily and with frustration, despite their otherwise balanced temperament.

Are you interested in many different things in life and like to stretch your fingers in many different directions like a tree stretches its branches? Do you like to move and do you enjoy physical exercise? Wood people are often good athletes; just as they are able to organize and plan their projects, they are also able to keep their bodies healthy and agile.

They are artists of survival who are able to adapt to any conditions and master their lives with strength and hope.

## The Language of Wood

Observe a tree or a bush and you will learn a lot about the essence and the language of wood. To grow and achieve its goals, the tree uses other elements: its roots sleep within the *earth,* drink *water,* and take in *metal* as trace element. Its leaves transform nutrients with the help of the sun's *fire.* We humans can also develop and use the qualities of other elements to fulfill our life plans.

The tree shows us how we can deal with obstacles and difficulties without losing ourselves. Supple and flexible, it moves in the storm and is still firmly rooted in the earth by its center, its trunk. It grows toward its goal, the sun.

Have you ever seen a tree whose trunk is curvy and knotty and twisted? Some trees have grown crookedly by being constantly blown in the same direction by strong winds. They teach us that we sometimes have to adapt to certain circumstances and have to decide which changes are necessary and how far we can or are willing to bend in order to reach our goal without breaking.

Trees in a forest grow in a certain order, even if they have not been planted in rows like on a plantation. In their competition to reach the light of the sun, the trees find their own order and balance. Observe their determination as they strive toward the sunlight. How they grow and unfold and stretch their branches. Watch how they bend in stormy winds and at the same time, they are firmly rooted in the Earth and connected to their trunks.

If you understand the language of the trees, the storms and changes in life will no longer take you off your path and away from your inner strength, but instead you will be able to live your dreams and realize your ideas with determination and purpose.

## Balance for Wood Nymphs

In order to best use your qualities as a wood nymph to everyone's benefit, it is wise to observe several things. Since wood people are interested in many things and always seek out new challenges and adventures, they may sometimes "overload" themselves and try to work on too many projects at the same time. If you stretch your branches in too many directions at once, they become thin and eventually might break off. Learn to know your limits and only take on as much as you can really finish.

Find out what nurtures your strong potential for growth, your talent for organization and your ability to express your constant flow of new ideas. Martial arts such as Taekwondo, Judo, Karate and Aikido strengthen your ability to assert yourself and keep your body flexible and supple. Maybe you like team sports, such as handball, volleyball, soccer, basketball, etc.? Or do you like to be a part of a group that campaigns for positive change? Organizations such as Greenpeace or environmental conservation groups have special youth groups where you can present your valuable ideas and comments and develop them further.

If you want to, you can also try out the rocking (see page 19) or magic eye (see page 21) exercises. Do what is fun and good for you and trust your strength!

You are walking along a pine-needle-covered forest path when you come to a little stream. It splashes happily down its bed. Where the drops jump over larger rocks, the water sprays white foam. You sit down on a flat, moss-covered boulder on the bank. Father Sun warms the air and makes the world around you glow bright and friendly. You enjoy the flowing quiet and look into the water…

Suddenly, you notice a little stone, about as big as the circle you can make with your thumb and pointer. You reach into the cold water and take it out. Its dark grey surface shimmers from the water. Fine white bands run across it and glitter in the sunlight. It feels smooth and round. The water droplets have worn away its edges over the course of time.

"Nice to meet you," you suddenly hear a voice say quietly in your head.

Puzzled, you look around, but no one is there. You hear soft laughter ring out and then vanish in the rushing of the stream.

"Stones are a path to knowledge," the voice continues.

The stone in your hand prickles pleasantly. It feels alive somehow.

"I *am* alive," the voice giggles. "If you want, I will tell you the secret of the seven faces of the stones."

You nod and the little stone in your hand speaks to you.

"We stones have been on this Earth since time eternal. Some

of us come from space and bring knowledge from distant stars and other worlds. If you learn the secret of our seven faces, you may hear many more of our stories and bits of wisdom in the course of your life."

The little stone lightly tickles the palm of your hand and continues: "The first face is the face of sounds. Did you know that all stones can speak and make sounds? We can sing and laugh, cheer and whine. Our songs can help other creatures harmonize their energies.

The second face is the face of sight. We stones can see you better than you can see yourself. We can also see things that are very distant or in the future. We can reveal secrets and treasures to you and show you shining worlds and the children of the stars. When you learn to see with the eyes of the stones, you can see everything. We stones can show you what will become of you. We can show you things lost and long forgotten.

The third face is the face of smell. We stones can smell scents that existed a hundred years ago. I can smell your scent and will remember it for the rest of my life. We stones can recognize other creatures by their smell. We save them and can find them again, no matter where they are.

The fourth face is the face of taste. We stones can eat. We nourish ourselves from light and many other different things. Many of us need water from time to time to survive, just like you humans.

The fifth face is the face of feeling. I can feel you and your being. I can feel if you are soft or hard, sick or healthy. I can feel inside your whole body. We can all do it, even without hands.

The sixth face is the face of perception. We stones can sense feelings. We sense whether you are sad or happy. And we can influence your feelings. For instance, we can make you feel better, lighter, and freer.

The seventh face is the face of consciousness. We stones are part of the great circle of life, just like all living creatures. We know that we are one with everything that surrounds us. We are all part of a great dream. Stones are like all living beings, we are simply much denser and vibrate slower."

You look at the little stone in your hand. It feels warm now and somehow not like a stone at all. The voice in your head is quiet now.

"Do you want to come with me?" you ask quietly.

A weak prickling flows through the palm of your hand and you hear the familiar voice once again, "I love the flowing of the water and feel most comfortable here in my stream. Visit me if you want and remember that many, many other stone friends await you on your life's journey."

Your heart suddenly feels happy and light. You thank your new friend and lay him back in the water. Deep within you, you can feel how much friendship, love and support flow toward you from the world of the stones.

Take this feeling with you and pay attention to the stone friends that you will meet along your path...

## Do You Belong to the Stone Family?

Stone people are not easily upset. Calm and patient, they observe the events around them. Too much confusion and activity just bounces off them. They would rather wait before quietly and slowly springing into action.

Members of the stone family can always be depended upon. They are good listeners and are often the calming influences in their families and circle of friends. Stone people can be found in many areas of life, as they are versatile and long sighted. They often have a healing and supporting effect on their surroundings. They enjoy the pleasant sides of life, whether food, massage or art, and they like to laugh.

## The Language of the Stones

Minerals and stones were the first living beings on Earth. Their circle of life takes much longer than that of humans. They are literally as old as stones and we can therefore learn a lot from their wisdom and experience. Back in the Stone Age, the healing powers of certain stones were discovered and since then, humans have used crystals and gemstones as protective and healing stones, for magic rituals and for seeing into the future.

Stones and crystals support you in difficult times in your life: when you are sick, frightened, unsure, having a fight or feel threatened. They speak to you in a very special way, sometimes quietly, sometimes loud and clear. Hold them in your hand or lay them on your body wherever it feels right for you; after a while, you will surely understand their language. You can also wear your special stone friends in a little clothe or felt bag around your neck.

The most powerful experience is finding stones in nature. In streams, on the beach, in the mountains and in caves – you can find stone beings in many places and in all forms and colors. If you want to take them with you, ask them first if they want to leave their spots! Like all of us, our stone friends also like to be asked before they are simply ripped away from their familiar surroundings. If you buy crystals or gemstones from a shop, ask about their exact care and cleaning instructions. Like every life form, they need special conditions to feel comfortable and stay healthy!

## Balance for Stone Faces

As a member of the stone family it does not bother you much when the storms of life bluster around you. You are as solid as a rock. But this also requires strength. Therefore, it is important that you take care of yourself and do things that replenish your energy. Otherwise, your quiet manner can turn into complacency. You may not notice your surroundings anymore and you may become dull. Breaking waves or winds that are too strong wear away the stone. Perhaps you like massages? Spoil yourself and do what feels good for you! Swimming, smooth, flowing movements in warm water help you relax and awaken the feeling within you that you are connected. Find ways to express yourself artistically that are fun for you and make you feel free without forcing you into a particular form, such as painting, photography, acting or making mosaics.

If you want, you can try the toning exercise (see page 8). It can deeply relax you and open you up.

As a stone person, it is especially good for you if your stone friends accompany you on your journey (this is, of course, true for all of us.) There are many different ways to choose "your personal" stone. It may simply come to you, perhaps as a gift. You may stumble upon it while walking around or you may notice it because of its color or shape or the way it feels. You can also go into a crystal shop and pick one out. It is important that you follow and trust your inner feeling and spontaneously reach in and grab whatever attracts you. You can choose the stone with your eyes by taking whichever one catches your eye. Or let your hand roam over the stones with your eyes closed and grab one when you feel the impulse. You can also research a certain stone in a book or ask an expert and find out which stone can help you with a specific problem or illness. I personally prefer the first two options, and I have found that the stones that you choose that way tend to be exactly the ones that fit your current situation.

It might be especially powerful for you to do the energy journey in the first chapter with "your" stone. Trust your inner feeling; your stone friends will guide and support you. Be good to them and find out exactly what they need to be happy and they will be your loyal companions and helpers.

# Metal

You are sitting in an alpine meadow. The last rays of sun warm the short, dry grass beneath you. Slowly, the clouds begin to change color and conjure magnificent images. They look like bright multi-colored flags waving over the sky. At this time of day, everything is preparing for the night. While the shining cloud ships in beautiful shades of red sail smoothly and slowly into the dark blue depth of the night sky, you walk along a path to a hollow in the rock. Inside, it is comfortably warm and protected from the wind. You light a little fire that bathes the room in a happily flickering light. In the glow of the fire, you see that the smooth cave walls shimmer like silver in some spots. You run your hand over the pleasantly cool surface. Little veins of silver course through the dark grey rock and glow in the firelight like glittering stars in the night sky.

Suddenly, you hear a soft sound. At the other end of the cave, you discover a little old woman. She is no bigger than your forearm. Her silver-grey hair frames her wrinkly brown face in wild waves. Her little eyes look firmly and directly at you.

"Sit down and join me," she says with a voice as clear as a bell.

Slowly, you go nearer. A bright silvery white light radiates from her body. She reaches into a wicker basket and takes out a large shiny grey nugget and gives it to you.

"I am the guardian of the ores," she explains and giggles quietly. "This stone has fine veins of silver running through it. Get to know it, feel it, speak to it and it will help you live your dreams."

The stone in your hand feels smooth and pleasantly cool. You feel the strong power and clarity that emanate from it. Images appear within your mind: the sharp blade of a sword gleaming in the sun. You see how it destroys things, but how it can also be used to protect. Iron nails, tools, horseshoes... You see many useful things made of metal that protect and build, but their unmovable strength can also destroy.

"Learn to use your metal power wisely and well, for yourself and others," you hear the guardian of the ores say. "Be strong, but not stubborn; be clear and determined, but not inconsiderate and hurtful. Learn to distinguish between these and you will be successful and happy."

Your silver stone suddenly starts to melt. Like glittering water, little streams of silver trickle through your fingers and gather in a puddle on the stone floor. All that is left in your hand is a crumbling piece of stone. Before your feet glows a little sea of silver.

The little woman laughs with a jingle and says, "To obtain the pure power of silver, sometimes you have to be soft and supple. Melt in the fire of life and leave the hard blocks of stone that burden you behind."

Her joyful laughter echoes on the walls of the cave. You look around and she has disappeared.

You thank her in your thoughts and know that you can always return to seek her help and advice.

## Do You Belong to the Metal Family?

Do you like it when everything is neat and tidy, orderly and clean? No bric-a-brac or unnecessary embellishments? Metal people generally appreciate a clear, Spartan[2] order. They have very unflinching personalities, are firm in their opinions and usually want to get their way. Determined, sometimes even stubborn and hard-headed, they go their own way. They prefer to rely on themselves and take care of things alone.

Metal is a very strong element. It can conduct electricity and its form can only be transformed by the power of fire. Thus, members of the metal family can carry strong energies within them and pass them on. They possess the strength to set things in motion. With determination, they stay "on the ball" and pursue their goals with focus and purpose.

If metal is your element, you probably do not rely on others very often. You have an exact idea of where you want to go and are ready to get there even without the support of others. Failures, disappointments or difficulties seldom scare you away; you will puzzle and work on it as long as you need to until you find a solution and succeed.

## The Language of Metal

Take a piece of metal, for instance a piece of jewelry, and hold it in your hand. How does it feel?

---

[2] The saying "Spartan order" comes from the very hard training and simple and minimal lifestyle of the people of Sparta, a city-state in ancient Greece.

Since metal is a very hard and inflexible element, it can take a while until you understand its language. Give yourself time! Feel how quietly and clearly the energy in the metal vibrates. Things made of metal teach us to look at ourselves and trust in our strengths and abilities. They show us how we can bring our inner visions out of us and make them reality by following our goals steadily and with determination without being influenced by obstacles that arise. When you are unsure about something, working with the element metal helps you become self-confident and determined.

### Balance for Silverlings and Gold Children

In order to keep a healthy balance, it is good for metal children to know how to open themselves to other vibrations. It is also helpful for them to recognize when the time has come to let go of something or a situation, for instance, when it is not working or not good for them. They tend to get deeply engrossed in something and hold tight to it stubbornly. In order to reach their "pure silver power", they have to become soft and melt in the fire of life. Doing things to this effect relaxes metal people and opens their eyes to the outside world.

If metal is your main element, it may be fun to try playing in an orchestra or band or dance with friends. Playing games together with others can widen your view: ball games, board games or simply playful activities like flying a kite, going for a bike ride or doing whatever you like will give you the opportunity to draw on your strengths while at the same time opening yourself to others.

If you feel stuck or you are having difficulties with others, it can help you to burn sandalwood in a fragrance lamp. Feel how strongly and firmly you are grounded within yourself. At the same time, allow yourself to melt in the fire of life's joys. See things from the lighter side; let go and let yourself be carried on the river of life.

Dance into an Inner Light...

Meditation is a simple and natural process in our lives. It is present in all things. A child lost in play is meditating. A hiker sitting on a rock high above sea level and looking out over the countryside is meditating. A dancer whose body seems melted into one with the music is meditating.

Little children spend long periods of time in a meditative alpha state – if we let them. Today, in our often hectic and over-stimulating daily lives, it is important to create (free) time to contemplate. Time to meditate and restore the balance between the demands of the outside world and inner spiritual strength is necessary for a balanced, self-determined life.

The consequences of our restless daily lives, which are often controlled by clocks, have almost become normal: children with superficial perceptions, children who are or "have to be" constantly in motion and have difficulty managing themselves, concentrating, and being sensitive; children who have lost awareness and respect. Children present various symptoms: allergies, hyperactivity, autism and many more. The need for balance, harmony and healing becomes more and more obvious. Different forms of meditation, autogenic training, breathing and physical exercises and immersing ourselves in nature help us feel the value of silence.

Meditation assists us to get to know our inner worlds and feel the essence of what we are. It enables us to have fundamental experiences with ourselves and others, with space and time and beyond. This is how the foundation is laid for an empathetic, altruistic and holistic consciousness.

We have seen that children and adolescents in particular react very directly and intuitively according to external impulses, especially if they are light, easygoing and fun for them. Initiating this atmosphere of playful light-heartedness is therefore one of the fundamental purposes of this book and the accompanying audio CDs.

Some children, or rather all people who have been too distracted from themselves and their inner needs seem, according to our observations, to be unable to enjoy silence and be calm. Sometimes they need "assistance." Experiences in which the consciousness is more collected, concentrated, and full of energy than in "normal" daily situations generally make entering a meditative state easier. Another proven tool for achieving this state is repetition. Children who want to hear a story over and over or look at a picture again and again automatically use this tool. For this reason, we designed the fantasy journeys in such a way that they can be repeated with variations and can become familiar to the listener.

Another way of entering the world of contemplation is through the ears. The ear is our most sensitive sensory organ. Animals with an especially well developed sense of hearing (e.g. dolphins, whales) also display especially loving and considerate social behavior.

*"The eye leads people into the world; the ear leads the world into the people."*[3] The music of Peter Prestel paints sound images that softly underline the fantasy journeys found in the second chapter, thus, stimulating the flow of one's own images. In his music, Peter uses original nature recordings (waterfall, streams, dolphins, birds, etc.), natural instruments (various percussion, string and wind instruments from indigenous cultures) and special frequency ranges to create a subtle resonance field within the listener and expand his or her consciousness. His

---

[3] Joachim Ernst Behrendt/Lorenz Oken, *Die Welt ist Klang – The World is Sound*

long-term experience and his knowledge of the meditative power and magic of sounds make this production one of many effective, insightful background scores.

The world of colors is also of great value on our way to achieving silence and toward ourselves. The sensitive illustrations by Wolfram Schulz underline important key aspects and create a positive, warm, light and inspiring atmosphere. At the same time, they leave room for individual visualization and fantasies.

Poems, stories, fantasy journeys, prayers, songs; they all fuel our imagination and let our creativity run free. The fantasy journeys in the previous chapters, in our experience, clear the way toward "the place of silence." They speak to the listener via the senses on several subtle levels to lead them into their inner worlds. Colors, music, text/language, images, elements and knowledge gained from different areas such as Qi Gong, autogenic training, NLP, hypnotherapy, and Reiki form the framework within which the listener's own content can grow and bloom.

# Possible Uses of this Book and the CDs

There are many different ways of using this little book and the CDs. The fantasy journeys from chapter 2 are available for free download or as audio CDs (ordering information see Appendix).

The journeys are suitable for individuals as well as for use in schools, public institutions, for therapeutic purposes, etc. Their special design makes them easy to adjust to individual needs: young children often orient themselves on the images in the book. The audio versions are practical and can be used in many situations; in the evenings, when you are out and about in the car, a bus, the train, or an airplane, and generally, whenever there is no "reader" available. The audio journeys lead the listeners step-by-step further and further into the deeper levels of their consciousness. There are purely instrumental passages to leave room for individual images and answers that want to dance into the light of consciousness. The deepest phase of relaxation is characterized by a longer passage without text, during which there is plenty of space for one's own visions and visualizations (see ⊚···········⊚ ). The duration of these "blank spots" is based on the experience we have gathered over the years. When reading the book aloud, the length of these pauses can be adapted to the individual needs of the person taking the journey.

***Reading the book and looking at the images:***

is particularly suitable

- for younger children
- when the reader wants to adjust his/her speed of speaking, pauses, etc. to the listener's pace
- for children who need something to "hold onto" and do not want to, or cannot go on a journey by themselves
- for children who cannot read yet; however, once the journey has been read to them, they are able to evoke it using the images/illustrations in the book

***Playing the guided fantasy journeys (audio CDs):***

is particularly suitable

- because the listener can repeat the journey with guidance and thus become more familiar with its course and possibilities
- because the listener can let him or herself be carried (the fantasy journeys are read aloud according to specific criteria that are based, among other things, on NLP and hypnotherapy as well as our own observations)
- when the guide (parent, sibling, teacher, educator, therapist, etc.) is not confident enough, does not have enough time or has other reasons for not wanting to read the journey aloud him/herself
- when the guide would also like to take the journey (e.g. in a school setting), in order to later include their own experiences with the meditation in potential (creative)

evaluations

- when there is no reader available (e.g. in a hospital)

***Playing the instrumental version (without a reader):***
is particularly suitable

- for repeating the journey alone when it is already internalized and familiar
- to leave room for new images emerging from within the listener
- to support and cultivate creativity
- to create a safe, familiar framework for new experiences
- when the reader wants to set his/her own accents (rhythm, inflection, emphasis, pauses, etc.) or better cater to individual needs

The possibilities listed here represent only a few of the options for playing around with the journeys – opportunities for using the book and CDs are as numerous and varying as our imagination, especially the children's imaginations.

# Observed Effects

- Through the journeys, children who disturbed class, could not sit still and had problems concentrating, found ways to express themselves which led to solutions for their "peculiar behavior."
- Teachers and educators successfully used the journeys to introduce and prepare for complicated, intensive learning processes (introduction of new topics, before school exercises, assessments, tests or exams, before presentations, etc.) and, for instance, when concentration began to wane during lessons.
- The meditations also helped bring inner solutions to physical symptoms such as headaches, stomachaches, allergies, asthma, etc. as well as psychological imbalances such as fear, lack of self-confidence and autism into the light of consciousness so that the external signals almost completely disappeared.
- Especially touching were the reactions of children in hospitals, some of whom were left fairly alone with their fears and pain. The journeys opened ways for them to reach their inner freedom and health.
- According to our experiences, the fantasy journeys provide an important opportunity, especially for very sick children who cannot or are not allowed to get up or even move, to balance out their situation and learn to cope with it — a

welcome "distraction" that guides them to the inner source of eternal life force and health that exists in us all.

- In our studies, we also came into contact with people who only felt their bodies when they were in pain. The meditations helped them to perceive themselves as a whole.
- And last but not least: It is always nice to observe the peaceful, relaxed and happy expressions and smiles on people's faces, when "returning" from the journeys.

# General Comments

- Fantasy journeys are a sensitive process that requires respect and empathy. The aspects mentioned here belong to the deepest parts of the personality and often originate relatively uncensored from the unconscious. According to our experiences children handle this process very differently. For some, it is important to have some kind of exchange after a journey during which they can share their images, wishes, fears, feelings and experiences. This exchange can take the form of a conversation – either individually or in a group – or a creative evaluation (e.g. painting, poetry, molding clay or putty, dance, pantomime).

- If the listener is very restless, it is recommended that you adapt the beginning of the fantasy journey to the mood and make it more lively (tone of voice, gestures, etc.). The journey will then automatically lead the listener to "stiller waters". The active meditations in the first part of the book are well suited for getting the children to tune in and practice concentrating.

- We observed that it is always important to engage the children according to their current mood and abilities. Only taking their situation seriously will then lead them to calmness.

- The meditations can generally be performed anywhere. However, many might find it helpful if the surroundings are quiet and, if there is little opportunity for external distractions. In our experience, it is nice to go to a quiet place in nature (forest, beach, river, lake...) to take the journey. Naturally grown environments, especially trees and water, strengthen the effectiveness and naturally enhance contemplation.

- There are, however, people who need a "foothold" and the security of a room around them in order to be able to let go and to immerse themselves! It is, therefore, very important and sensible when choosing a location (if such a choice is possible) to find out what the child's/children's individual needs and abilities are.

- The same is true for the individual layout of the journeys, for instance, through pauses in speaking to leave room for inner pictures. Observe the person taking the journey and feel what "fits" them. Posture, facial expression and gestures can provide you with insightful hints in this regard. Let yourself be guided by the children.

- We are often asked if the children should close their eyes. In our experience, the answer to this question depends on the age of the children as well as other influencing factors. Younger children are often not yet ready to keep their eyes closed for longer periods of time. They do, however, usually have the ability to sink deep into the meditation despite any apparent external focus (e.g. playing with stones, etc. during the meditation). Older travelers sometimes find closing their eyes unusual at first, but after getting used to it, they generally find it helpful for diving deeper into their own world of images.

- Simply offer the children the option of closing their eyes if they want to.
- We recommend playing the audio versions fairly quietly. Our ears perceive external stimuli much more intensely in a meditative state, much like when we are falling asleep. Turning the volume up too loud can thus often have a disturbing effect. We have found that it is easier for the travelers to find calmness when the playback is relatively quiet. The music and voice have been mixed so that they keep their presence and effectiveness even when they are turned down.

Have fun, enjoy yourself and have a good journey!

*We are always grateful to receive comments and accounts of your experiences that we can use to further our work:*

birgitbaader@gmail.com

# About The Illustrator

Wolfram Schulz is an artist with heart and soul. He loves to play with colors, patterns and images. His artistic creations make walls and rooms come to life. They bring the jungle into the children's room, the sickroom, and the playroom. He paints anything from the vastness of the ocean in offices, to the orange-colored sandy calmness of the desert in living rooms, entrance halls or waiting rooms.

The wonderful and colorful diversity of nature is his source of inspiration, and he brings its beauty and healing power into our interiors. Wolfram wants to touch, move, inspire and give you something you can take with you on your soul journey.

Since 1998 Wolfram has worked as a freelance wall designer and artist and has transformed many rooms into an oasis of wellbeing. His paintings have been displayed to the public in over 50 exhibitions throughout Europe.

Wolfram currently lives with his wife in Switzerland.

www.wolfram-schulz.ch

# About The Musician/Composer

Peter Prestel loves music and constantly lives in a world of sound and wonder. Playing many instruments, Peter is always keen to explore new ways to create sounds, to perceive sounds and to transform sounds. He is interested in finding out more about the various ways in which the power of music has been used in different cultures throughout time.

By creating wonderful, subtle soundscapes and by using the special healing powers of sound, Peter weaves a musical magic carpet on which you can fly into other realities. His music can lead us deep inside; it can set us free and help us to connect with our inner healing powers.

Peter has explored many different styles of music. Besides his classical training on various instruments including the guitar, piano, bass and flute, he plays wonderful music using his hands, plastic tubes, shells, sticks, stones, glass, and anything around him.

He is open to listening and tuning in to the many vibrations surrounding us. Thus, his music invites you to perceive sound in a multicolored and varied way that will immerse you in the healing world of sound.

# About The Author

Birgit Baader is interested in many aspects of life. She loves talking and listening to animals, plants and crystals, and loves collecting stories, knowledge and information to share with others. She sees the world as a vast playground for everyone who is passionate about scooping from the rich pool of life's treasures.

From an early age, Birgit has been interested in connecting to other realities. She has communicated not only with birds, horses and dolphins, but also with all kinds of "fantasy beings". Birgit loves spending time in Nature, swimming in the ocean, or enjoying the wild bush of Aotearoa, where she currently lives with her family. Collecting exciting stories and knowledge from different cultures and life forms around the world are just some of the areas she likes to explore.

Birgit has written and published books and articles in various print and online media as well as produced films and CDs. Her intention is to raise awareness for the great sacred web that connects all life. She strives to strengthen the feeling of interconnectedness and "oneness", and to share tools for self-awareness and self-empowerment. With extrasensory and interspecies communication, she believes we can plunge into a universal pool of wisdom and knowledge that reaches far beyond the physical limits of our own species.

Birgit is available for lectures and "playshops" in the fields of "interspecies communication", "journeys into inner sources of power with children", "natural birth", and "alternative learning concepts".

**You can contact her at: birgitbaader@gmail.com.**

# Appendix

The fantasy journeys from chapter 2 are available as audio versions.

For free download or to order the Audio CDs please visit:
**http://www.birgitbaader.com/books.html**

| | | |
|---|---|---|
| 1. | **The Inner Dolphin** | **16:16** |
| 2. | **The Butterfly Woman** | **19:53** |
| 3. | **Dolphin Journey** | **18:47** |
| 4. | **At the End of the Rainbow** | **19:39** |